100
Sweet Treats
by & for
QUILTERS

Ann Hazelwood

100

Sweet Treats
by & for
QUILTERS

> Take time to
> smell the
> flowers
>
> Patches Redwork Club · St. Charles, MO ·
> February 2009

Ann Hazelwood

American Quilter's Society
P. O. Box 3290 • Paducah, KY 42002-3290
www.AmericanQuilter.com

TAKE TIME TO SMELL THE FLOWERS, detail, made for the author
by Patches Redwork Club, St. Charles, MO

COVER QUILT: FIESTA FLORIBUNDA II, detail, made by Anne
Lullie, Lake in the Hills, IL

Located in Paducah, Kentucky, the American Quilter's Society (AQS) is dedicated to promoting the accomplishments of today's quilters. Through its publications and events, AQS strives to honor today's quiltmakers and their work and to inspire future creativity and innovation in quiltmaking.

EXECUTIVE BOOK EDITOR: ANDI MILAM REYNOLDS
GRAPHIC DESIGN: ELAINE WILSON
COVER DESIGN: MICHAEL BUCKINGHAM
PHOTOGRAPHY: CHARLES R. LYNCH, UNLESS OTHERWISE NOTED

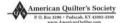

American Quilter's Society
P. O. Box 3290 • Paducah, KY 42002-3290
www.AmericanQuilter.com

Additional copies of this book may be ordered from the American Quilter's Society, PO Box 3290, Paducah, KY 42002-3290, or online at: www.AmericanQuilter.com.

Library of Congress Cataloging-in-Publication Data
Hazelwood, Ann Watkins.
  100 sweet treats by & for quilters / by Ann Hazelwood.
    p. cm.
  ISBN 978-1-57432-662-8
  1. Desserts. I. Title. II. Title: One hundred sweet treats by & for quilters.
  TX773.H343 2010
  641.8'6-dc22

                                2009052487

Printed and bound in Mexico

Dedication

There are many sweet quilters in this industry, and I have come across many of them in my 30 some years in the business.

Dellene Olendorff of St. Charles, Missouri, is one of the sweetest quilters I have ever known. She has been an employee, and is a great cook, quilter and friend. Her sweetness continues to be enjoyed by many family members and friends. Therefore, as a thank you, this book is dedicated to her.

REMEMBERING SUMMER, detail, Pamela A. Conklin, O'Fallon, IL

Contents

Introduction

Quilters know how to do many things well besides making quilts. Their creativity spreads to many areas like gardening and cooking delicious food to share.

As everyone loves wonderful treats to make and eat on special occasions or for a "pick me up" on an ordinary day, it seemed natural to match quilters, quilts, and sweet treats!

It was delightful contacting these great quilters for a short and sweet recipe to share with you, and I thank them all. Their great quilts reflect their quilting talent, and nothing complements a beautiful quilt like a sweet treat!

Some of the quilts are scattered throughout the book to make it pretty, rather than matched by maker and recipe, so it's a treasure hunt, too! I hope you enjoy the special treats—edible and visual—chosen just for you.

OPPOSITE: NATIVE HABITAT, detail, Libby Lehman, Houston, TX PHOTO: Libby Lehman

Bars

Chocolate Brittle

Place a layer of foil in an 11x16x1 pan.

Place 40 soda crackers on foil.

Combine 1 cup butter *(not margarine)* and 1 cup brown sugar.
    Boil for 3 minutes.

Pour over crackers.

Bake at 350 degrees for 5 minutes or until crackers float.

Remove from oven and sprinkle 1 heaping cup chocolate chips
    over crackers.

Bake for 30 seconds to melt chocolate.

Spread melted chocolate over crackers.

Sprinkle 1 cup nuts on top.

Cut into bars while still warm.

Janet Steadman, Langley, Washington

OPPOSITE: FLIGHT PLAN, detail, Janet Steadman, Langley, WA PHOTO: Frank Ross

one

Lemon Surprise

Dissolve 1 small package lemon gelatin
    in 1 cup boiling water.
Add 3 Tbsp lemon juice. Let cool.
Mix:
    1 can chilled Milnot® milk product
    8 oz cream cheese
    1 cup sugar
    1 tsp vanilla
Add to gelatin.
Pour into pre-made graham cracker
    crumb crust in a 9x13 pan.
Top with extra graham cracker
    crumbs and refrigerate.
Cut into serving size squares when
    set.

Anna Poore, Florissant, Missouri

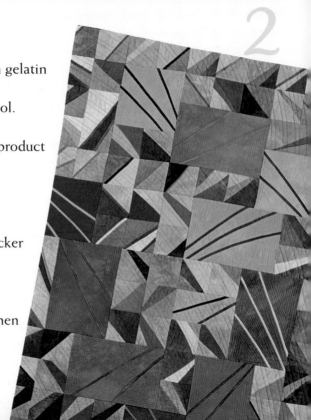

Oaties

3

Mix:

    2 cups sugar
    3 Tbsp cocoa
    ½ stick margarine
    ½ cup milk
    a pinch of salt

Bring to a boil over medium heat, stirring often.

Boil for 1 minute.

Remove from heat and add ½ cup peanut butter and 3 cups quick-cooking oats.

Place mixture on a buttered 9x13 cookie sheet and chill in refrigerator.

Cut into squares to serve.

Terry David, St. Charles, Missouri

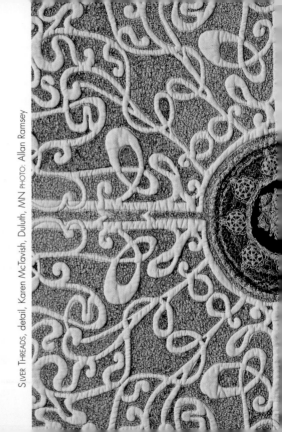

SILVER THREADS, detail, Karen McTavish, Duluth, MN PHOTO: Allan Ramsey

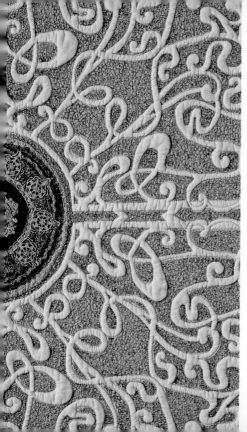

Pecan Pie Bars

Makes 36

4

Combine 2 cups unsifted flour and ½ cup powdered sugar.

Cut in 1 cup cold margarine or butter until crumbly.

Press firmly onto the bottom of a 9x13 baking pan and bake 15 minutes.

Beat 1 can sweetened condensed milk, 1 egg, and 1 tsp vanilla.

Stir in 1 package (6 oz) almond brickle chips and 1 cup chopped pecans.

Spread evenly over crust.

Bake at 350 degrees for 25 minutes or until golden brown.

Store uncovered in the refrigerator.

Alice Kay Arnett, Laramie, Wyoming

four

Bishop Bread Coffee Cake

Mix:
> 1½ cups flour
> 2 cups brown sugar
> ½ tsp salt
> ½ cup vegetable oil

Reserve ½ cup of the mixture for topping.

To the remaining mixture add:
> 1 tsp baking powder
> ½ tsp baking soda
> 1 tsp cinnamon
> 1 egg
> 1 cup sour milk*

Beat briskly until well blended.
Pour batter into a greased and floured 9x13 pan.
Sprinkle with reserved topping.
Bake at 350 degrees for about 30 minutes or until toothpick inserted in center comes out clean.

Mark Lipinski, Califon, New Jersey

To make sour milk, add 1 Tbsp white vinegar or lemon juice to 1 cup milk and let stand 5 minutes.

Chocolate Zucchini Bread

Sift:

    1 cup white bread flour
    ¼ cup dark cocoa powder
    ½ tsp baking powder
    ½ tsp baking soda
    1½ tsp cinnamon
    ½ tsp ginger

Mix 2 eggs, ½ cup olive oil, ½ cup honey, and 1 tsp vanilla.

Add the wet ingredients to the dry ingredients and mix well.

Stir in 1 cup shredded zucchini, ½ cup dark chocolate chips, and ½ cup chopped walnuts.

Pour batter into greased 4x9 bread pan and bake 45 minutes at 350 degrees.

Debra Danko, Grand Blanc, Michigan

ABOVE: CRYSTALS, Mark Lipinski, Califon, NJ PHOTO: Mark Lipinski

Cream Cheese Croissants

Gently unroll 1 can Pillsbury® Crescent dinner rolls.
Keeping joined, press into bottom of greased 9x13 pan.
Cream 8 oz cream cheese and ½ cup sugar.
Spread evenly on crescent layer.
Layer second can of crescent rolls over cream cheese.
Sprinkle a mixture of ¼ cup sugar and 1 Tbsp
    cinnamon evenly on this layer.
Pour 1 stick melted butter evenly on top
    and bake at 375 degrees for 20
    minutes.

Virginia Kopfinger, Defiance, Missouri

FANTASIA, detail, Nancy J. Peters, Wildwood, MO PATTERN: Spiral Lone Star by Jan Krentz

seven

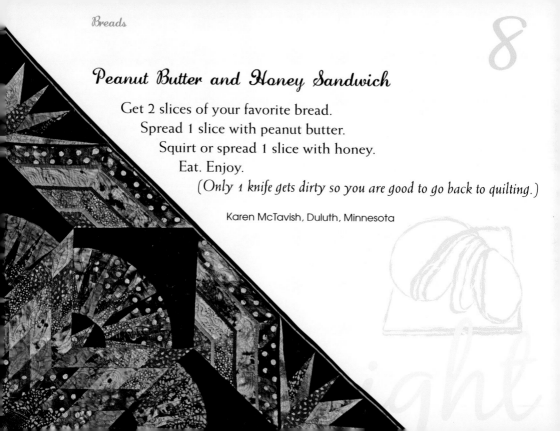

Peanut Butter and Honey Sandwich

Get 2 slices of your favorite bread.
Spread 1 slice with peanut butter.
Squirt or spread 1 slice with honey.
Eat. Enjoy.
(Only 1 knife gets dirty so you are good to go back to quilting.)

Karen McTavish, Duluth, Minnesota

9

Violet's Crescents

Cream ½ lb butter and ½ cup powdered sugar with 1 egg yolk.

Add 2 cups flour, 1 cup walnuts, and ¼ tsp vanilla.

Beat until well blended.

Shape into crescents about the size of a miniature Tootsie Roll® candy.

Bake on an ungreased cookie sheet at 350 degrees for 10 minutes or until bottoms start to lightly brown.

Let cool for 10 minutes before rolling in additional powdered sugar.

Good with strawberries and ice cream.

Nancy Peters, Wildwood, Missouri

Brownies

Apple Brownies

Mix:

 1 cup flour
 1 cup sugar
 ½ tsp salt
 ½ tsp baking powder
 Optional: 2 tsp cinnamon

Add:

 1 small-to-medium peeled and
  chopped apple
 2 beaten eggs
 ¼ cup melted margarine
 ½ cup raisins
 1 cup chopped walnuts

Mix well. Batter will be stiff.
Spread batter in a greased
 9x13 baking dish.
Bake 30–40 minutes at 350 degrees
or until edges are golden brown.
Remove from oven and cool slightly.
Cut into squares or bars.

Bonnie Zabzdyr, Wright City, Missouri

Bodacious Brownies

Follow directions on your favorite brownie mix. (*I like Ghirardelli® Triple Chocolate Brownie Mix.*)

Put half the mix in pan and cook for 10 minutes.

Remove from oven and layer 1 Hershey® Symphony® candy bar (*any flavor*) on top, breaking it up.

Add rest of brownie mix.

Bake for remainder of time listed on the package.

You can cut these while warm if you use a plastic knife. Otherwise, let cool before cutting.

Libby Lehman, Houston, Texas

MIDNIGHT STAR BLUMING, detail, Milly Blumer, O'Fallon, MO

Brownie Pizza

Grease a 14-inch pizza pan.

Prepare a family-size brownie mix according to the package directions.

Spread batter in pan.

Bake at 350 degrees for 18 minutes or until edges are set.

Sprinkle partially baked brownie with desired toppings such as chocolate chips, white chocolate chips, nuts, and chopped candy bars.

Top with lots of miniature marshmallows and bake another 8 minutes. Watch carefully so marshmallows just barely get brown.

For frosting: Blend ½ stick butter, 2½ Tbsp milk, and 1¾ Tbsp cocoa and heat until boiling.

Remove from heat and add ½ box (8 oz) powdered sugar. Mix until smooth. Add ½ tsp vanilla.

Tip: If you put the frosting in a bag, you can swirl it over the brownie.

Milly Blumer, O'Fallon, Missouri

Chocolate Decadence

Break or cut cooled, pre-baked brownies into
1-inch cubes.

Layer half in a large, clear, glass serving
bowl.

Layer ½ cup prepared chocolate mousse
mix.

Repeat the brownie and mousse layers.

Top with 1 cup whipping cream with 2 Tbsp
sugar whipped until firm peak stage.

Sprinkle with 6 oz chopped Heath® English
Toffee bar and serve.

*(If you really want to be decadent, use 2 packages
of mousse mix with just one layer.)*

Kathy Delaney, Overland Park, Kansas

14

German Chocolate Brownies

Bake your favorite commercial brownie
    mix as directed. *(I prefer Ghirardelli®*
    Triple Chocolate Brownie Mix.)
Bake as directed in a 7x11 pan.
Let cool approximately 30 minutes.
Spread with an entire can of Duncan
    Hines® Creamy Home-Style Coconut
    Pecan Frosting.
Refrigerate overnight before serving.

Alice Werner, St. Charles, Missouri

OPPOSITE AND RIGHT: RED HOT WOMEN OF DESIGN, details,
Kathy Delaney, Overland Park, KS
PATTERN: Women of Design BY BARBARA BRACKMAN

Miracle Brownies

Combine:

> 1½ cups flour
> ⅞ cup cocoa
> 1 tsp salt
> 1 tsp baking powder
> 1⅓ cups shortening
> 4 eggs
> 4 tsp vanilla
> 2 cups sugar
> 1 cup chopped nuts

Mix until well blended.

Pour into a 9x13 pan sprayed
> with cooking oil.

Bake at 350 degrees for about
> 25 minutes.

Beverly Dunivent, Olympia, Washington

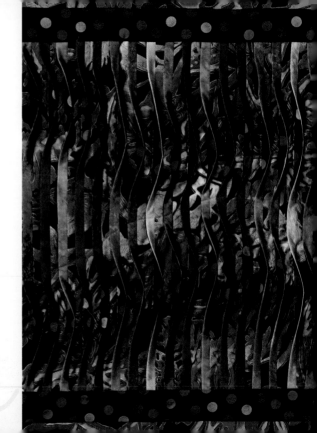

Moosewood Fudge Brownies

Cream ½ lb softened butter with 1¾ cups packed light brown sugar and 5 eggs.

Add ½ tsp vanilla extract.

Beat in 5 oz melted bitter unsweetened chocolate and 1 cup flour.

Spread into a 9x13 pan and bake 20–30 minutes at 350 degrees.

Wanda Kruse, St. Louis, Missouri

LEFT: THE PHANTOM FISH, detail, Alice Werner, St. Charles, MO

Sarah's Simply Sinful Dessert

Bake 1 brownie mix of your choice.
Cut brownies into 1-inch cubes.
Prepare 2 cups fresh berries such as
    strawberries.
Layer berries, brownies, and
    whipped cream in parfait glasses.
Garnish with a fresh berry and mint
    leaf.

Lisa Erlandson, Gainesville, Texas

Your Own Quick Brownie

Mix 2 Tbsp brownie mix of your
    choice and 1 Tbsp vanilla yogurt
    in a small microwave safe bowl,
    such as a custard-size bowl.
Microwave 1 minute at full power.
A small treat just made for you!

ABOVE RIGHT: MAPLE LEAF, detail, Beverly Dunivent,
Olympia, WA PATTERN: class with Ruth McDowell

Mickey Wittliff, Clarence, New York

Cakes

Angel Food Favorite

Put a slice or cubes of angel food cake in a serving dish.

Pour a lot of fresh strawberries (or your favorite berry) over the cake so that a lot of the juice soaks into the cake.

Top off with Cool Whip® Whipped Topping or freshly whipped cream.

Sheila Steers, Eugene, Oregon

RIGHT: LARGO BEARS, detail, Alice Kay Arnett, Laramie, WY PATTERN IINSPIRED BY: Sally Collins
PHOTO: Alice Kay Arnett

nineteen

Broken Glass Jell-O Cake

Serves 8 - 10

Prepare 1 package each of JELL-O® Orange, Cherry, and Lime Flavor Gelatin separately, using 1 cup hot water and ½ cup cold water per package.

Pour into 3 separate 8x8 dishes and chill until firm.

Heat 1 cup pineapple juice and ¼ cup sugar until sugar dissolves.

Remove from heat and dissolve 1 package of JELL-O Lemon Flavor Gelatin into the hot liquid.

Add ½ cup cold water and chill until syrupy.

Mix 1 cup graham cracker crumbs with ¼ cup melted butter or margarine.

Press the crumb mixture smoothly over the bottom of a 9-inch springform pan.

Whip 2 cups whipping cream and fold into the lemon mixture.

Cut the other 3 JELL-O flavors into cubes and fold into whipping cream.

Pour into springform pan and chill 8 hours.

Becky Rogers, Los Osos, California

Butter Pecan Cake

Combine:

    1 box of Betty Crocker® Super-
        Moist® butter pecan cake mix

    1 can of Betty Crocker Rich &
        Creamy coconut pecan frosting

    4 eggs

    1 cup oil

    1 cup water

    1 cup chopped pecans

Mix together and pour into a Bundt
    pan.

Bake for 1 hour at 350 degrees.

Cheryl See, Fayette, Missouri

SPOOLING AROUND, detail, Bonnie Zabzdy
Wright City, MO

twenty-one

Chocolate Cement Cake

Stir together 3 times:
- 1½ cups flour
- 1 cup sugar
- 3 Tbsp cocoa
- 1 tsp salt
- 1 tsp baking soda

Spread evenly in a 6x10 or 8x8 ungreased cake pan.

Make 3 indentations in the flour mix.

Add 1 Tbsp apple cider vinegar in one well, 1 tsp vanilla in one well, and ⅓ cup vegetable oil in one well.

Pour 1 cup of cold water over all and combine.

Batter will be thin. Be sure to mix in the dry ingredients, especially in the corners.

Bake at 350 degrees for 35 minutes or until toothpick inserted in center is clean.

Cool on rack and frost if desired or add whipped cream and fresh raspberries.

Since this cake is dense, it can be served right out of the pan.

Diane Gaudynski, Waukesha, Wisconsin

OPPOSITE: SHADOWS OF UMBRIA, detail, Diane Gaudynski, Waukesha, WI PATTERNS: Stellar Delight by Plum Creek Patchwork, Johanna Wilson

Chocolate Pudding Cake

Prepare a devil's food cake mix according to directions and set aside. Do not bake.

Mix 1 cup brown sugar and 1 cup powdered cocoa in a 9x13 pan.

Stir in 2 cups water and 1 cup miniature marshmallows.

Spoon unbaked cake mix into pan.

Top with 1 cup broken nuts.

Bake at 350 degrees for 40–45 minutes.

Serve warm with ice cream.

Phyllis Nelson, Independence, Missouri

Cola Cake

Combine 2 cups flour and 2 cups sugar.

Heat 2 sticks butter, 3 Tbsp cocoa, and 1 cup cola to boiling.

Pour over flour and sugar mixture and mix thoroughly.

Add:

½ cup buttermilk

2 beaten eggs

1 tsp baking soda

1 tsp vanilla

1½ cups marshmallows

This will be a thin batter with marshmallows floating on top.

Bake in a greased 10x15x1 jelly roll pan for 30–35 minutes at 350 degrees.

For icing heat:

½ cup margarine

3 Tbsp cocoa

6 Tbsp cola

16 oz confectioner's sugar

Add 1 cup pecans.

Spread icing on cake while it is still hot.

Karen Guthrie, Marshall, Missouri

Dad's Wacky Cake

Mix into an 8- or 9-inch square pan:
- 1½ cups flour
- 1 cup sugar
- 3 Tbsp unsweetened cocoa
- 1 tsp baking soda
- ½ tsp salt

With your index finger, make 3 holes in the flour mixture.

Pour 5 Tbsp melted butter in the first hole, 1 Tbsp vinegar in the second, and 1 tsp vanilla in the third.

Pour 1 cup of water over all.

Stir well until combined.

Bake at 350 degrees for 25–35 minutes.

Immediately top cake with 1 cup mini-chocolate chips and bake 2–3 minutes longer until chips are soft.

Spread chocolate over top of cake. Good with ice cream.

Amy Korn, Westerville, Ohio

FANS OF TIME, detail, Amy Korn, Westerville, OH PATTERN: Carol Doak

Dirt Cake

Blend 16 oz cream cheese.

Add 2 cups confectioner's sugar and 16 oz Cool Whip® Whipped Topping. Set aside.

Make 2 packages (6 oz) instant chocolate pudding. Set aside.

Crush 20 oz Oreo® cookies.

Layer items in a large flower pot or ceramic pot without a hole in the bottom, or cover bottom hole with parchment paper or foil, starting and ending with crushed cookies.

Mix a few candy gummy worms throughout each layer.

Arrange a few silk flowers on top and/or sprinkle with a few more gummy worms.

Serve with a shovel-like serving piece.

Jean Douglas, St. Charles, Missouri

SUBTLE SIXTIES, detail, Linda M. Roy, Knoxville, TN

Dump Cake

Dump 1 can crushed pineapple in a 9x13 pan.
Dump 1 can cherry pie filling over pineapple.
Pour 1 package yellow cake mix over pineapple and cherry mixture.
Sprinkle 1 cup nuts over all.
Slice 2 sticks butter over the nuts.
Bake at 350 degrees for 1 hour.

Linda Roy, Knoxville, Tennessee

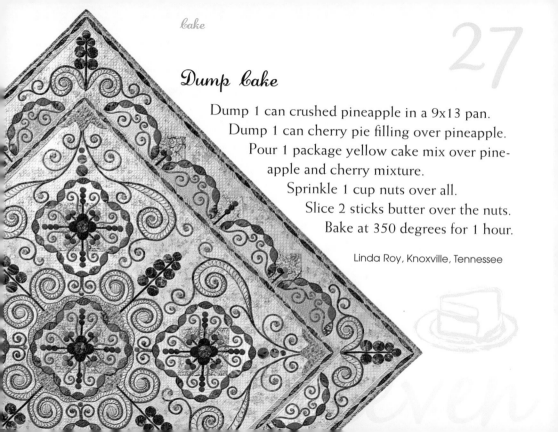

German Crumb Cake

Cut 2 cups brown sugar and 2 cups
    flour into 1 cup butter.
Reserve 1 tamped cup of this mix-
    ture.
Sift:
    1 tsp soda
    1 tsp baking powder
    1 tsp salt
    2 tsp nutmeg
    2 tsp cinnamon
Add to the sugar mixture.
Add 2 unbeaten eggs and 1 cup sour
    milk*.

Pour into a greased 9x13 cake pan.
Sprinkle the top with reserved
    mixture.
Bake 35–40 minutes at 350 degrees.

Jill Bryant, Chesterfield, Missouri

*To make sour milk, add 2 Tbsp white
vinegar or lemon juice to 1 cup milk. Let
stand 5 minutes.*

Gingerbread Yule Log

Use 1 package Anna's Ginger Thins®
cookies or another flavor.

Whip 1 pint whipping cream with
½ cup sugar and ½ tsp vanilla or
use 16 oz Cool Whip® Whipped
Topping.

Make a log by stacking the cookies
alternately with a dollop of cream
and laying the stack on its side.

Make a smaller limb of broken cookies coming off to one side.

Cover it all in whipped cream.

Crush broken cookies and sprinkle
on top.

Slice on the diagonal.

Kim Ritter, Houston, Texas

UNDER THE SEA, Jill Bryant, St. Louis, MO and Nancy Brown,
San Jose, CA PHOTO: Jill Bryant

Grandma Stanton's Strawberry Shortcake

Sift together 2 cups flour, 1 Tbsp baking powder, 3 Tbsp sugar, and ¾ tsp
    salt.
Cut in ½ cup Crisco® All-Vegetable Shortening with pastry blender until
    slightly lumpy.
Add 1 beaten egg and ½ cup milk.
Stir until blended.
On a greased cookie sheet, drop dough in 6–8 mounds about 2 inches apart.
Bake at 450 degrees about 12–15 minutes or until lightly brown.
Cut off the top of the shortcake and add strawberries that are sliced and
    lightly sugared.
Add the top of the cake and more berries.
Top with whipped cream.

Linda Hunter, Lockport, New York

Kelsey's Cinnamon Cake

Combine 1 box spice cake mix and 1
package instant French vanilla pudding mix.

Add 2 cups of milk, ¾ cup cinnamon
chips* (saving ¼ cup for topping),
and ½ cup chopped pecans.

Stir and pour into 9x13 pan.

Sprinkle reserved chips on top.

Bake at 350 degrees for 30–35 minutes
until center is done.

Ann McNew, Winfield, Missouri

*Located in the baking aisle and from online
baking sources.*

POPPY: A REMEMBRANCE ROSE, detail, Annette M.
Hendricks, Grayslake, IL PHOTO: Annette M. Hendricks

Laisy Daisy Cake

Serves 9

Beat 2 eggs, 1 cup sugar, and 1 tsp vanilla until thick and lemon-colored.

Combine 1½ cups flour, 1 tsp baking powder, and 1 tsp salt.

Add to egg mixture.

Heat ½ cup milk and 2 Tbsp butter until butter melts.

Add to batter. (Batter will be thin.)

Pour into greased 9-inch square pan.

Bake at 350 degrees for 20–25 minutes.

For frosting, blend ¾ cup brown sugar, ½ cup melted butter, 2 Tbsp light cream, and 1 cup shredded coconut. Spread on warm cake.

Broil about 4 inches from heat 3–4 minutes or until top is slightly browned.

Delores Keaton, Pacific, Missouri

AHOYA, detail, Dolores Keaton, Pacific, MO
PHOTO: Dolores Keaton

Lemon Poppy Seed Cake

Mix together:

    4 eggs
    ½ cup oil
    1 package instant lemon or vanilla pudding
    ¼ cup poppy seeds
    1 cup hot water

Beat for 1 minute.

Slowly add 1 box yellow or lemon cake mix and
    continue beating for 4 minutes.

Grease and flour baking pans (see below).

Bake at 350 degrees in 2 medium cake pans or 5
    small loaf pans for 35–40 minutes.

If using a Bundt pan, bake for 1 hour.

When done and cool, sprinkle with powdered sugar.

Annette Hendricks, Grayslake, Illinois

Oatmeal Cake

Pour 1¼ cups of boiling water over 1
cup of quick oats.

Add 1 stick (½ cup) of margarine
and let it stand for 20 minutes.

Mix:

    1 cup white sugar

    1 cup brown sugar

    2 eggs

    1⅓ cups flour

    1 tsp baking soda

    ½ tsp cinnamon

    ½ tsp nutmeg

Stir together and bake at 350 degrees for 35 minutes.

While cake bakes, mix:

    6 tsp soft margarine

    ½ tsp vanilla

    1 cup chopped nuts

    ½ cup sugar

    ¼ cup evaporated milk

    1 cup coconut

Spread on baked cake.

Broil for a few seconds until coconut
browns.

Bobbie Kuschel, Maryland Heights, Missouri

OPPOSITE: IN APPLE BLOSSOM TIME, detail, Diane Shink,
Montreal, Canada
PATTERN: inspired by Cotton Queen Patterns #34

Russian Tea Cakes

½-inch balls make 5 dozen

1-inch balls make 2 dozen

Combine:

    1 cup butter or lard

    ½ cup confectioner's sugar

    2¼ cups sifted flour

    ¼ tsp salt

    1 tsp vanilla

    ¾ cup finely chopped pecans

Refrigerate until cool.

Form into balls.

Place on non-greased cookie sheet.

Bake 14–17 minutes at 400 degrees.

While hot, roll in confectioner's sugar.

Cool and roll in sugar again.

Dellene Olendorff, St. Charles, Missouri

Strawberry Puree Cake

Prepare and bake 1 strawberry cake mix in a 9x13 pan.
When cool, poke several holes with the handle of a wooden spoon.
Puree 1 package sweet frozen strawberries. Pour over cooled cake
while still in the pan.
Combine 1 box instant vanilla pudding mix with 1½ cups milk.
When partially set, fold in 12 oz Cool Whip® Whipped Topping.
Spread topping mixture on cake.
Refrigerate for 2–3 hours before
serving.

Michael Marsh, Marshall, Missouri

RIGHT AND OPPOSITE: COUNTRY PATCHWORK VILLAGE,
Michael D. Marsh, Marshall, MO

Apple Crisp

Peel and slice 6 apples into a greased
9x9 ovenproof dish.

Mix 1 cup rolled oats, 1 cup flour,
and 1 cup brown sugar.

Melt 1 cup butter or margarine and
pour over dry ingredients.

Pour mixture over apples and
combine well.

Bake at 350 degrees for 40 minutes.

Serve with vanilla ice cream or
whipped cream.

Diane Shink, Montreal, Canada

Apple Lattice Fruit Bake

Stir together ¾ cup brown sugar, ⅓ cup water, and 2 Tbsp flour until smooth.

Add 6 cored and sliced Granny Smith apples, ½ cup chopped pecans, and ½ cup chopped dried mixed fruit.

Toss the fruit mixture in the brown sugar mixture until well coated.

Pour into a 9x13 baking dish.

Cut 1 sheet thawed frozen pastry into ten 1-inch strips with a pizza cutter.

Lay 5 of the strips over the apples lengthwise. Cut the remaining 5 strips in half.

Place the 10 smaller strips over the apples widthwise to create the lattice.

Mix 1 Tbsp white sugar and ¼ tsp cinnamon. Sprinkle over lattice.

Bake at 375 degrees until the apple mixture is bubbling and the lattice is golden brown, about 40–45 minutes.

Jan Cherry, Belleville, Illinois

OPPOSITE: FEEDSACK MAGIC, detail, Hallye Bone, St. Louis, MO PHOTO: Hallye Bone

Cobblers

Brown Betty

39

Put 4 cups of very thinly sliced apples
    into a lightly buttered baking dish.
Mix:
    1 tsp cinnamon
    a dash of nutmeg
    a dash of salt
    ¾ cup flour
    1 cup sugar
Add 1 stick softened butter or marga-
    rine. Rub mixture into the apples.
Bake at 350 degrees about an hour or
    until golden brown.
Serve warm with a slice of cheddar
    cheese over the top.

Mary Ann Kemper, Troy, Missouri

Fruit Crisp

Serves 6

Peel and slice 6 medium tart apples or other
    fruit. (If using rhubarb, add ½ cup sugar.)
Spread in an 8x8 baking dish.
Mix:

    ½ cup softened butter
    ¾ cup brown sugar
    ½ cup flour
    ¾ cup quick cook oatmeal (uncooked)
    1 tsp cinnamon
    ½ tsp nutmeg

Spread over the fruit.
Bake for 40 minutes at 375 degrees until apples
are tender.
Top with whipped cream or heavy cream.

Caryl Schuetz, Indianapolis, Indiana

DANCING LILIES, detail, Caryl Schuetz, Indianapolis, IN

Great Depression Cobbler

Serves 4

Melt ¼ cup butter in an 8x10 baking dish.

Pour a can of pie filling onto melted butter.

Mix:

    1 cup sugar

    1 cup flour

    2 tsp baking powder

    ¼ tsp salt *(optional)*

    ¾ cup milk

Stir until smooth and pour over pie filling.

Bake at 350 degrees for 40 minutes or until dough is brown.

Hallye Bone, Town and Country, Missouri

Great Grandma's Berry Cobbler

Mix together:

> 1 cup flour
> ½ cup sugar
> 1 rounded tsp baking powder
> 1 Tbsp shortening
> a pinch of salt
> ½ cup milk

Pour this batter evenly into a 9x11 baking dish.

Top with 1 cup frozen or fresh blueberries, blackberries, or Oregon Marionberries.

Sprinkle with ½ cup sugar.

Pour 1 cup (¾ cup if using frozen berries) boiling water over the top of fresh berries.

Bake at 400 degrees for 30 minutes until golden brown.

Sandra Leichner, Albany, Oregon

Magic Peach Cobbler

(Substitute cherries, apples, or blackberries)

Melt 1 stick butter in a 9x13 glass baking dish.
Combine:

    ½ cup sugar

    1 cup flour

    1½ tsp baking powder

    ¾ cup milk

Pour mixture over melted butter, but do not stir.
Place 2–3 cups peeled and sliced peaches on top
    of batter.
Sprinkle with another ½ cup sugar.
Sprinkle nutmeg over top.
Bake at 350 for 35 minutes or until golden
    brown.

Mary Ellen Pratt, St. Charles, Missouri

POPPY SOLILOQUY, Sandra Leichner, Albany, OR

Peach-Blueberry Cobbler

6 – 8 servings

Peel and slice 4 large peaches. Coat with sugar. Mix with 1 cup blueberries.

Mix:

- 1 cup sugar
- 1 cup white flour
- 2 tsp baking powder
- 1 tsp salt

Melt ½ cup butter.

Add 1 cup milk.

Pour butter mixture into dry ingredients and stir until smooth.

Pour batter into an 8x12x2 greased glass baking dish.

Spread fruit evenly on top of batter.

Bake at 350 degrees for 50 minutes or until golden brown.

Serve warm with whipped cream.

Phyllis Hatcher, Annapolis, Maryland

Peach Crisp

Serves 6–8

Place 4 cups sliced peaches in an 8x8 greased pan.
Sprinkle with 2 Tbsp water and ¼ cup sugar.
Combine 1¼ cups Bisquick® Original Pancake
   and Baking Mix, ½ cup sugar, and ¾ tsp
   cinnamon.
Beat 1 egg.
Pour slowly over dry mixture, stirring
   constantly until crumbly.
Spread mixture over peaches.
Pour ¼ cup melted butter or
   margarine over all.
Bake at 400 degrees for 25
   minutes or until brown.

Jean Biddick, Tucson, Arizona

ABER'S GIFT, detail, Jean Biddick, Tucson, AZ

Peach Kuchen

Mix 1 cup flour and ½ cup diced cold butter until it resembles cornmeal.

Put mixture into a lightly greased 9x9 baking pan and pat out evenly, pressing firmly.

Arrange 4–5 peeled and sliced fresh peaches in overlapping rows.

Mix together 3 Tbsp sugar and ¾ tsp cinnamon and sprinkle on top of fruit.

Bake 18 minutes at 400 degrees.

Remove from oven.

Reduce heat to 375.

For top custard layer, beat 1 cup half-and-half and 2 eggs.

Pour the cream mixture over the fruit and bake for 45 minutes.

Let stand 30 minutes before serving cool or warm.

Barbara Hammond, Saddlebrooke, Arizona

Cold Desserts

Angel Cake Roll-up

Prepare an angel food cake mix as directed. Do not bake.

Spread into wax paper-lined jelly roll pan coated with cooking spray.

Bake 30–35 minutes at 350 degrees.

Turn onto towel sprinkled with powdered sugar, then roll towel and allow to cool to shape.

While cake is cooling, prepare 1 small package of instant vanilla pudding.

Blend in 8 oz Cool Whip® Whipped Topping and 8 oz cream cheese.

When completely cooled, unroll cake, spread on filling and re-roll.

Chill before serving.

Joan Abbitt, St. Charles, Missouri

RIGHT: HOME FIRES BURNING, detail, Pat Owac
St. Louis, MO PHOTO: Pat Owac

Banana Split Cake

Mix 1 stick melted margarine, ½ cup powdered sugar, and 2 cups crushed vanilla wafers.

Pack on the bottom of a 9x13 cake pan.

Beat 2 egg whites, 1 stick soft margarine, and 2 cups powdered sugar.

Spread over first layer.

Arrange 3–5 sliced bananas on top.

Cover with 1 large can crushed pineapple.

Top with 16 oz Cool Whip® Whipped Topping.

Sprinkle with nuts and/or cherries.

Freeze 15 minutes, then refrigerate until time to serve.

Irene Mueller, Ballwin, Missouri

RIGHT: Button Up, detail, Irene Mueller Miller, Ballwin, MO

Chocolate Eclair Cake

Mix 2 small packages French vanilla instant pudding with 3½ cups
whole milk.

Beat for 2 minutes.

Blend in one 8 oz container Cool Whip® Whipped Topping.

Line a 9x13 pan with graham crackers, breaking to fit if necessary.

Pour ½ the pudding mixture over the crackers. Add a second layer of
crackers.

Add the rest of the pudding mixture. Add a third layer of crackers.

Spread 1 can of chocolate frosting on top of the last layer.

Refrigerate for 8–24 hours.

Diana Brock, Williamsville, New York

Frozen Strawberry Dessert

For crust, combine:

- ¼ cup brown sugar
- 1 cup flour
- ½ cup butter
- ½ cup chopped nuts

Mix and bake in a 9x13 pan for 10–15 minutes at 350 degrees.

Crumble when cool and sprinkle back into the same 9x13 pan.

Combine:

- 10 oz thawed frozen strawberries
- 2 egg whites
- ½ cup sugar
- 1 Tbsp lemon juice

Beat egg whites till frothy, then add sugar mixture.

Add strawberries and lemon juice after beating for 20 minutes.

Fold in 1 cup whipping cream, then fold this mixture into strawberries.

Pour over crust and freeze for 4 hours.

Top with whipped cream before serving.

Klonda Holt, Lee's Summit, Missouri

fifty

Kool Dessert

Mix:

> 16 oz Cool Whip® Whipped
> Topping
> 5 sliced bananas
> 1 large can pineapple chucks
> 1 can whole berry cranberry
> sauce
> 1 cup walnuts

Pour into a 9x13 dish and freeze.

Remove a few minutes prior to
serving.

Cut into squares.

Edith Idleman, Bella Vista, Arkansas

BIRD SANCTUARY, Deana D. Brock, Williamsville, NY
PHOTO: Deana D. Brock, PATTERN: Black-capped Chickadee by
Paula Minkebige, Crossed Wing Collection

fifty-one

Orange (or Key Lime Pie) Balls

Crush 12 oz vanilla wafers into crumbs and add:

    1 cup powdered sugar
    ½ cup softened butter
    ½ cup orange juice *(limeade concentrate for Key Lime recipe)*
    ½ tsp vanilla *(almond extract for Key Lime recipe)*

Smush until ingredients are evenly distributed.

Roll the batter into 1-inch balls, then roll in ¼ cup powdered sugar to coat. *(Use non-latex plastic gloves so the batter doesn't stick.)*

Keep refrigerated until time to eat.

Chris Moline, Naperville, Illinois

Pennsylvania Cheesecake

Beat:

    2 packages (8 oz each) ⅓ less-fat cream cheese

    1 cup egg substitute

    ⅓ cup sugar

    ½ tsp almond extract

Pour into a 9-inch greased pie plate or round pan.

Bake 30–35 minutes at 350 degrees.

Cool 20 minutes.

Mix 1 cup light sour cream with 3 Tbsp sugar and
    1 tsp vanilla.

Spread on top of the cream cheese mixture.

Bake 10 minutes at 350 degrees.

Refrigerate when completely cooled.

Top with fruit.

Pat Owac, St. Louis, Missouri

LEFT: THE MILER, detail, Christine A. Moline, Naperville, IL

The P.T.A. Green Salad

Mix:

    1 package pistachio pudding
    1 can crushed pineapple with
       syrup
    ½ cup chopped nuts
    10 or 12 oz of Cool Whip®
       Whipped Topping
    2 cups small marshmallows
Cool in the refrigerator for 2–3
    hours before serving.

Donna Baker, Fayette, Missouri

THISTLE, Mary Ellen Pratt, St. Charles, MO
PHOTO: Mary Ellen Pratt

DAWN STARS, Jane C. Hall, Raleigh, NC
PHOTO: Jane C. Hall

Quick Biscuit (Cookie) Tortoni

Soften ½ gallon vanilla ice cream.
Working quickly, mix in:

   1 cup toasted slivered almonds
   1 cup coconut
   1 cup currants
   1 jar maraschino cherries, chopped
   1 tsp rum or vanilla extract

Spoon the mixture into cupcake papers
   lined up on a cookie sheet with sides.
Freeze until firm.
Vary the amounts of nuts/coconuts/raisins
   to taste.

Jane Hall, Raleigh, North Carolina

Snowball Sundaes

Serves 4

Dribble ½ cup chocolate chips into 4 clear dessert glasses.

Add a scoop or two of the best quality vanilla ice cream.

Pour ¼ cup crème de menthe liqueur per glass over the ice cream.

Top with ½ cup divided coconut sprinkles.

Top each sundae with a maraschino cherry.

Cindy Brick, Castle Rock, Colorado

RIGHT: ANNIVERSARY QUILT, detail, Karolyn Reker, Carterville, GA PHOTO: Karolyn Reker, PATTERN: Bride of Tulip Valley by Jeanna Kimball

White Trash Sundae

Line the bottom of a 9x13 pan with ice cream sandwiches (use part of 2 boxes of 6-count).

Cover with ½ bottle caramel sauce, toasted pecans, and 8 oz Cool Whip®.

Repeat layers. Freeze.

Cut and serve in squares.

Jamis Kresyman, Shrewsbury, Missouri

cookies

Banana Split Cookies

Combine:
- ½ cup powdered sugar
- 2 eggs
- ½ cup cream cheese
- ½ cup oil
- 1 tsp vanilla extract
- 1 small package instant banana pudding

Mix well, then add:
- ½ tsp baking soda
- ½ tsp cream of tartar
- 2 cups flour
- ⅛ tsp salt

Stir in ½ cup chopped pecans.

Chill 1 hour. Shape into balls one inch in diameter.

Put on cookie sheet and make a thumb impression in each cookie.

Place a maraschino cherry in each impression.

Bake 10–12 minutes at 350 degrees.

As cookies cool, melt chocolate chips to drizzle on top of cookies, or sprinkle with powdered sugar.

Cheri Hofeldt, Warrensburg, Missouri

Chef Caviar's Chocolate Chip Oatmeal Cookies 59

Mix until really creamy:

    1 Crisco® Butter Flavor
        All-Vegetable Stick
    1 stick (½ cup) butter
    1 cup white sugar
    1 cup brown sugar

Mix in 2 large eggs, 2 Tbsp milk, and 2 tsp vanilla.

Sift:

    2 cups flour
    1 tsp baking powder
    1 tsp baking soda
    1 tsp salt
    1 tsp nutmeg
    2 tsp cinnamon

Add dry ingredients, one cup at a time, to the butter and sugar mixture.

Stir in 2 cups old-fashioned oatmeal, 1 bag Ghirardelli® Semi-Sweet Chocolate Chips, and 1 cup chopped pecans or walnuts.

Cover with plastic wrap and refrigerate for about 1 hour.

Place about 24–30 scoops of dough onto a greased cookie sheet.

Bake at 350 degrees for 8–9 minutes. Cookies will be slightly underbaked.

Laurie Malm, Fernandina Beach, Florida

fifty-nine

Chocolate Drop Cookies

Spray cookie sheets with PAM®
  no-stick cooking spray.
Melt 12 oz bitter Ghirardelli® 60%
  Cacao Bittersweet Chocolate
  Chips and ¼ cup butter.
Add 1 can sweetened condensed
  milk.
Add 1 cup flour.
Drop by teaspoon onto cookie sheet.
Bake at 350 for 6–10 minutes, being
  careful not to overbake.

Anne Lullie, Lake in the Hills, Illinois

LEFT: BASEBALL BATIK, Laurie I. Malm, Fernandina Beach, FL

sixty